Facts About
Rivers

DONNA BAILEY

STECK-VAUGHN
LIBRARY
Austin, Texas

How to Use This Book

This book tells you many things about rivers and lakes. There is a Table of Contents on the next page. It shows you what each double page of the book is about. For example, pages 10 and 11 tell you about "The River Valley."

On most of these pages you will find some words that are printed in **bold** type. The bold type shows you that these words are in the Glossary on pages 46 and 47. The Glossary explains the meaning of some words that may be new to you.

At the very end of the book there is an Index. The Index tells you where to find certain words in the book. For example, you can use it to look up words like tributaries, rapids, floodplain, and many other words to do with rivers.

Published in the United States in 1990 by Steck-Vaughn Co., Austin, Texas, a subsidiary of National Education Corporation.

© Macmillan Publishers Ltd 1989
Artwork © BLA Publishing Limited 1987

All rights reserved. No reproduction, copy or transmission of this publication may be made without written permission.

Material used in this book first appeared in Macmillan World Library: *Rivers and Lakes*. Published by Macmillan Children's Books

Printed and bound in the United States
1 2 3 4 5 6 7 8 9 0 LB 94 93 92 91 90

Library of Congress
Cataloging-in-Publication Data

Bailey, Donna.
  Rivers / Donna Bailey.
    p. cm. — (Facts about)
  Summary: Describes aspects of rivers and lakes, including their history, benefits to humanity, pollution, and conservation.
  ISBN 0–8114–2510–X
  1. Rivers — Juvenile literature. [1. Rivers. 2. Lakes.]
I. Title. II. Series.
GB1203.8.B33   1990
910'.0216'93—dc20

89-26132
CIP
AC

Contents

Introduction	4	The Ganges	28
Water on the Move	6	The Mississippi	30
Rivers and Waterfalls	8	The Rhine	32
The River Valley	10	The Murray	34
The Flat Lands	12	The Amazon	36
Life in a River	14	How Lakes Are Made	38
Rivers in Hot Countries	16	The Great Lakes	40
Rivers in Flood	18	The African Lakes	42
River Power	20	Harming Rivers and Lakes	44
People and Rivers	22		
Rivers, Lakes, and Dams	24	Glossary	46
The Nile	26	Index	48

Introduction

We all need water to live. The chart shows that most of the Earth's water is in the salty oceans and seas.

A lot of water is frozen in the huge ice caps of the North and South Poles. Only a tiny amount of water comes from rivers.

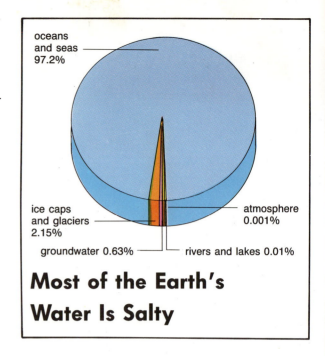

Most of the Earth's Water Is Salty

the Antarctic ice cap

the Nile River

People, animals, and plants need **fresh water** to stay alive.

The picture shows trees and plants growing beside the banks of the Nile River in Egypt.
Farther from the river there is no water, so the land becomes a desert.

People get most of their water from rivers and lakes, or from **groundwater** that comes from wells.
Rain falls from the clouds and helps to fill rivers and lakes with water.

Water on the Move

Water is always moving, on the Earth, in the air, and in the sea.

We call the movement the **water cycle**. The picture shows how water moves.

Groundwater and water from streams and rivers flow downhill to the ocean. The hot sun shines on the oceans and lakes and the water **evaporates.** It turns into **vapor** that rises into the sky until it meets the cold air. The cold air **condenses** the vapor and changes it back into drops of water, which fall as rain from the clouds. Snow falls when the air is very cold.

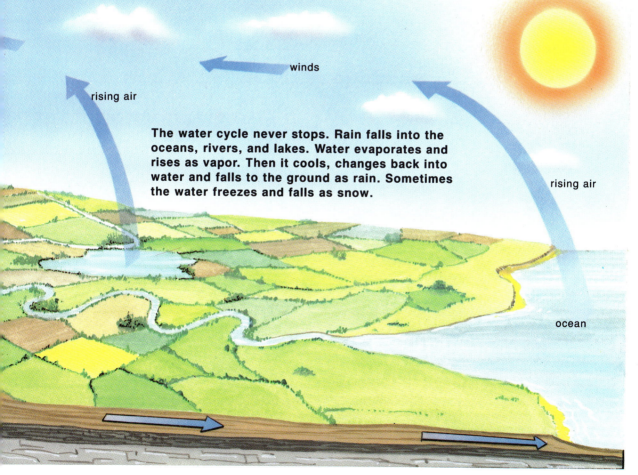

The water cycle never stops. Rain falls into the oceans, rivers, and lakes. Water evaporates and rises as vapor. Then it cools, changes back into water and falls to the ground as rain. Sometimes the water freezes and falls as snow.

Rivers and Waterfalls

a V-shaped valley made by a young river

The start of a river is called its **source**.

Many rivers start as **springs** in high mountains. Springs make streams that flow rapidly down the sides of the mountain. The streams or **tributaries** join together to make a fast-flowing river.

The river carries loose stones along in its **bed.** The water and stones cut a channel through the rocks to make a V-shaped valley.

If the river flows over areas of hard and soft rocks, the water wears away the soft rock by **erosion,** leaving the hard rock jutting up in the riverbed, making **rapids.**

When the river comes to a steep drop it falls over the edge as a waterfall.

If the river flows over a layer of hard and then a layer of soft rock, the water wears away the soft rock first, leaving a lip or cliff of hard rock. The river tumbles over the cliff, making a waterfall.

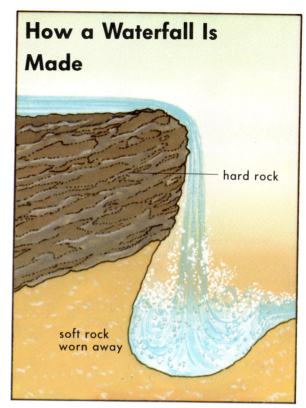

How a Waterfall Is Made

hard rock

soft rock worn away

Niagara Falls

The River Valley

As the river flows down the valley, the ground gets less steep, so the river slows down. It gets wider and its water is calm.

The river is joined by more streams as it winds its way around the hills. Towns are built on the riverbanks.

how a river meanders

The soil and stones in the river erode its banks so the river now begins to swing from side to side, or **meander** in gentle loops. The river drops soil and stones on the inside bends where it flows more slowly, and erodes the outer banks where it flows much faster.

an eroded riverbank

The Flat Lands

As the river reaches the end of its journey, the land becomes flat. The river is very wide now and it meanders its way slowly in huge loops across the **floodplain.** The river still carries tiny bits of stone and soil with it, called **silt.**

heavy rain makes floods

crops grow well on the floodplain

The river slows down before it enters the ocean, and forms an **estuary.** The river drops its silt in the estuary to make marshy **mud flats.** The ocean washes a lot of the silt away.

Some rivers drop so much silt that it builds up and makes new islands. Then the river fans out to make new channels through the **delta.**

Life in a River

In the upper **reach** of a river the water flows fast. Trout can swim against the flow of water, while the **larvae** of insects cling fast to the rocks among the weeds, called **algae.** Birds called dippers feed on insects or larvae.

More plants and weeds take root in the calmer waters of the middle reach. Fish like the catfish, or barbel, live near the bottom and feed on mayfly larvae, snails, and plants.

In the calm lower reach, herons wade in the shallow water to catch fish like the pike, while below the surface we find shrimps, clams, and even turtles.

Rivers in Hot Countries

Rivers that flow through **tropical** countries are full of fish and plants.

Tropical rivers have many **predators** that wait in the water to catch food. Electric eels and electric catfish kill their **prey** with electric shocks. Piranha fish are very fierce and attack anything swimming in the water.

Other predators wait on the muddy riverbanks to catch their prey.

alligators live in muddy swamps

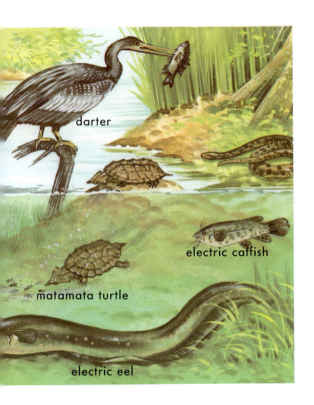

The darter catches fish with its pointed beak.

Matamata turtles hide in the muddy water and look like lumps of dead wood. If a fish comes near, the turtle snaps it up.

Hippos spend most of their day in the river. They are not predators, but feed on grass and other plants on the bank. Hippos can swim well, and can hold their breath for a long time underwater.

hippos in an African river

Rivers in Flood

Most floods are caused by heavy rain. Rivers get so full that they burst their banks and the water pours out over the nearby farms and roads.

Some rivers flood at the same place each year, so the banks of these rivers are built up above the flood level to form **levees.**

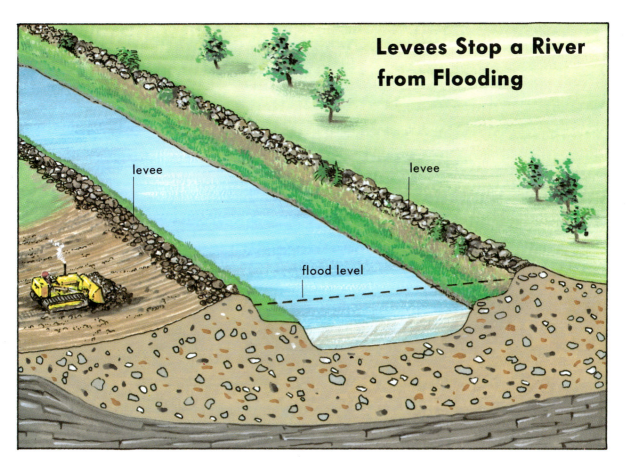

Levees Stop a River from Flooding

When the flood waters go down, the land is wet and often needs to be **drained**. **Dikes** and canals are dug to carry the water away.

Much of the Netherlands is below sea level, so the sea is held back by a dike. Machines pump the water off the land into canals.

farmland drained by dikes

River Power

The power of moving water is used to turn water-wheels.
The force of water falling onto an **overshot wheel** makes it turn much faster than an **undershot wheel**.

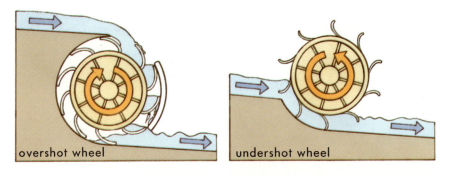

overshot wheel   undershot wheel

undershot wheels being used for irrigation in Portugal

Hoover Dam

Special water-wheels called **turbines** are used to make electricity in modern **hydro-electric** power stations.

Water from the mountains is held back in a **dam**. **Sluice gates** in the dam wall are opened and water pours into the turbine, making it turn very fast. This drives the machine that makes electricity.

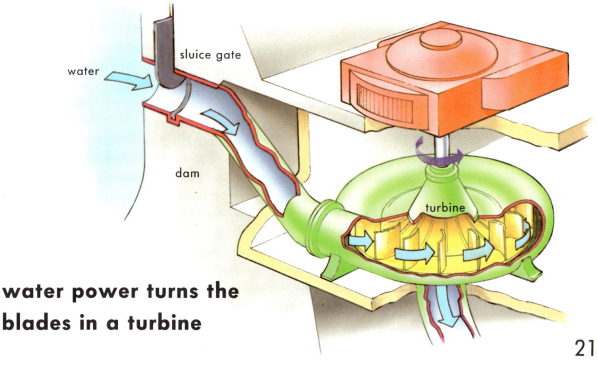

water power turns the blades in a turbine

People and Rivers

Many countries use rivers like roads.
   The Amazon River in Brazil flows through thick jungle where there are few roads, so people travel by river.
   In hilly areas, it is easier to take heavy goods by river than by road. The picture shows two barges full of goods making their way up the Yangtze-Kiang River in China.

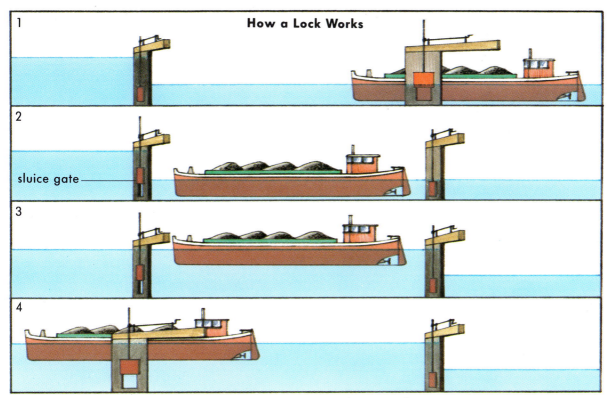

How a Lock Works

sluice gate

People have built towns on the banks of rivers, and bridges to cross from one side to the other.

Where the river is steep, locks are built to help barges go up the river.
1. The barge goes into the lock at the lower level.
2. The lock gates close and the sluice gates open.
3. The barge rises to the higher level of the river.
4. The lock gates open and the barge leaves the lock.

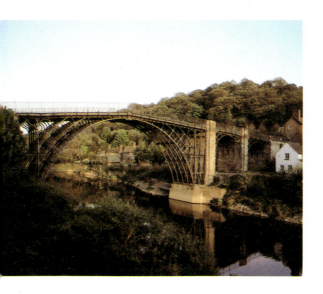

the first iron bridge

Rivers, Lakes, and Dams

Our map shows the longest rivers and the largest lakes in the world. The Nile River is the longest river.

The Ten Longest Rivers	Length (miles)
Nile, Africa	4,144
Amazon, South America	4,048
Mississippi-Missouri, North America	3,759
Yangtze-Kiang, Asia	3,721
Ob-Irtysh, Asia	3,199
Amur, Asia	2,899
Zaire, Africa	2,717
Hwang Ho, Asia	2,699
Lena, Asia	2,645
Mackenzie, North America	2,635

The Ten Largest Lakes	Area (sq m)
Lake Superior, North America	31,822
Lake Victoria, Africa	26,830
Lake Huron, North America	23,012
Lake Michigan, North America	22,401
Lake Tanganyika, Africa	12,700
Great Bear Lake, North America	12,276
Lake Baikal, Asia	11,781
Lake Malawi (Lake Nyasa), Africa	11,431
Great Slave Lake, North America	11,032
Lake Erie, North America	9,941

The Great Lakes of North America form the world's biggest group of lakes.

The deepest lake is Lake Baikal in the Soviet Union which is nearly 5,712 feet deep. The world's biggest **reservoir** is Lake Volta in Ghana, covering 3,275 square miles.

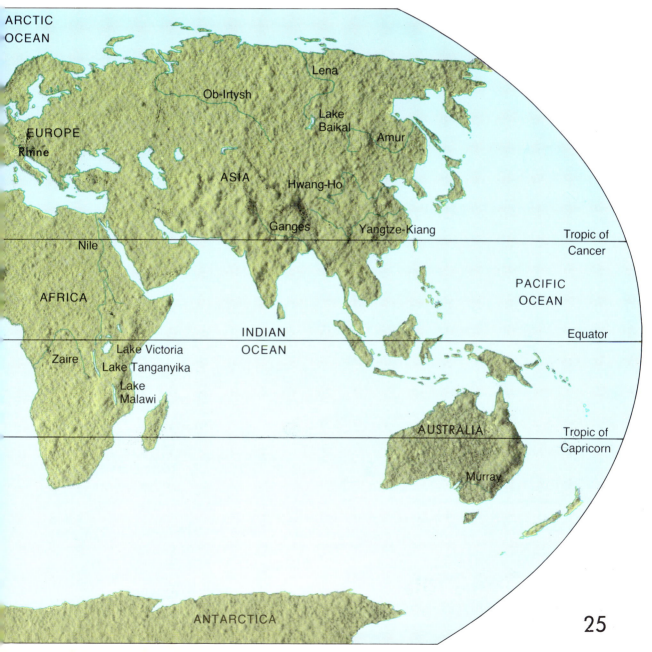

25

The Nile

farmers irrigate their fields with water from the Nile

The Nile in Egypt is the world's longest river. It has a **fertile** delta at its mouth where the river branches into many streams.

If you look down on the Nile Valley from a plane, you can see two strips of green, fertile land on each side of the river where crops are grown. Beyond the green bands lies the desert.

The Nile used to flood every year and dropped rich silt at the delta. Now the flood waters are held back by the new Aswan High Dam, which provides water and hydro-electricity for Egyptian homes and industries.

The temples of Abu Simbel in our picture stand beside the Nile. They were built over 3,000 years ago by Rameses II, a king of Egypt.

the Aswan High Dam

The Ganges

The Ganges is 1,550 miles long and flows through India into Bangladesh. It meets the Brahmaputra River at Bangladesh, where it forms the largest delta in the world.

Many people believe the Ganges is a holy river, and make a **pilgrimage** to Varanasi to bathe in its waters.

bathing in the river at Varanasi

The Ganges has been used for trade and travel for many hundreds of years.

The people of Patna use its water for dyeing cloth.

Many people make their living by fishing, while others grow rice in the floodplain and the delta.

fishing in the Ganges

The Mississippi

The Mississippi is the longest river in the United States. It travels 2,348 miles to flow into the Gulf of Mexico. It carries huge amounts of silt along with it. Special machines called dredgers are used to clear a way through the silt in the shallow water.

Early traders found that flat boats were best for traveling through shallow water in the Mississippi River.

The picture shows the oil refineries that now stand on the banks at Baton Rouge, with strings of coal barges chugging past along the river.

The Mississippi has been used to carry goods since it was first explored in 1681. Furs were carried down from the north in barges, and the tobacco and cotton grown in the south were taken back up the river to Canada.

Steamboats began to appear over 150 years ago, and are still used today to carry tourists.

The Rhine

The Rhine is 820 miles long. It rises in Switzerland, crosses western Europe, and empties into the North Sea. It carries millions of tons of cargo every year.

Our picture shows barges, trucks, and a freight train, three kinds of transportation found in the Rhine Valley.

a Rhine barge on the Europa canal

There are big coalfields where the
Rhur joins the Rhine in West Germany.
The Rhine is used to carry the coal,
oil, and other heavy goods to the many
cities and factories along its banks.

The Rhine then flows on into the
Netherlands, where it forms a delta.
Here the river splits into channels
as it makes its way to the sea.
The main channel is the Lek River
which flows through the huge port of
Rotterdam out into the North Sea.

The Murray

At 1,200 miles long, the Murray River is the longest river in Australia. It flows from the Australian Alps down to the Indian Ocean, in South Australia.

the Murray River

Lake Eucumbene

the Lady Augusta

The *Lady Augusta* was the first steamboat to travel up the Murray to the point where it meets the Darling River.

A huge **irrigation** project, the Snowy Mountain Project, has made it possible to farm the dry lands along the Murray Valley.

Dams were built for the Snowy Mountain Project to make hydroelectricity. The dams formed lakes like Lake Eucumbene, which is shown in our picture.

The Amazon

The Amazon flows through South America for 4,048 miles. It begins in the Andes in Peru and flows east through Peru and Brazil. It flows through thick **rain forest** where some of the trees are 200 feet high. There are few roads, so people travel by river.

the Amazon River

a riverside market

The Amazon is so big that it carries one-fifth of the world's fresh water. It is so wide and deep that large ships can sail 2,300 miles from the river mouth to Iquitos in Peru.

Our picture shows the floating dock at Manaus, Brazil, which was built over one hundred years ago for ships to carry rubber along the Amazon. Today the port is not as busy and ships carry nuts, vegetable oils, and wood instead of rubber.

How Lakes Are Made

A lake is a large hollow filled with water by rain, streams, and rivers.

Many lakes were formed during the **Ice Age**, when sheets of ice covered the Earth, and heavy **glaciers** moved slowly across the surface, scooping out hollows in the rocky surface.

ice and rocks scoop out a valley

the ice melts and drops the rocks

the Akosombo Dam in Ghana with Lake Volta behind it

There was once a volcano in the place where we can see the **crater lake** in our picture.

Some enormous lakes have been made by building dams across rivers, such as the Bratsk Reservoir in the Soviet Union, which holds more water than any other lake in the world.

The Great Lakes

The five Great Lakes lie on the border between the United States and Canada. Our map shows the border and where we can find Lake Superior, Lake Michigan, Lake Huron, Lake Erie, and Lake Ontario, and the diagram shows how deep the lakes are.

Lake Superior is the largest freshwater lake in the world.

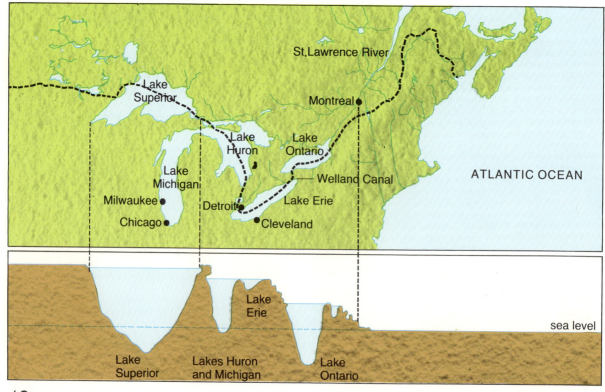

a cargo ship enters a lock on the Seaway

The water from the Great Lakes flows into the St. Lawrence River.

A series of locks and canals on the river called the St. Lawrence Seaway were built so that ships can sail all the way up the St. Lawrence River from the Atlantic to Lake Superior.

In the winter the Seaway is frozen for 120 days.

a tanker on the river

The African Lakes

The map shows some of the large lakes that can be found on the eastern side of Africa. Among these lakes are Lake Victoria, Lake Tanganyika, and Lake Malawi.

The lakes form natural barriers between several African countries. Lake Kariba in our picture is often visited by tourists.

Lake Kariba

42

The lakes provide water for growing rice and other crops.

Many of the people who live around the lakes on the eastern side of Africa earn a living by fishing or farming. The picture shows a group of people preparing for a day's fishing on Lake Tanganyika. The lake is 420 miles long.

Harming Rivers and Lakes

Many rivers and lakes have become dirty from **chemicals** poured into them by towns and factories. **Untreated sewage** from our homes can spoil the water in rivers and lakes. When a river or lake becomes **polluted,** the plants and fish die.

a river polluted by chemicals and waste

Many countries are trying to stop the pollution of their rivers and lakes. Industries are not allowed to pump their dirty waste into the rivers.

Scientists collect samples of water, animal, and plant life to test them for chemicals and waste matter. Some people are trying to find new ways of making water clean and safe.

Glossary

algae very simple plants with no leaves, roots, or stems.
bed a river or stream bottom.
chemicals substances that can change when mixed with others to make a different substance.
condenses when something changes from gas to liquid.
crater lake a lake that has been formed in a hollow in the shape of a bowl.
dam a strong wall built to hold back a river.
delta a fan–shaped area of land formed by the mud, sand, and stones dropped by a river at its mouth. The river divides into many channels as it flows through the delta to the sea.
dikes the name given to drainage ditches and thick earth walls built to hold back water and control floods.
drained when water has been pumped or channeled away from the flooded land.
erosion wearing away of land by water, ice, or weather.
estuary the wide mouth of a river where it meets the sea.
evaporates when something changes from liquid to gas.
fertile soil where plants grow well.
floodplain the flat area on either side of a river over which it floods.
fresh water water that does not contain salt.
glaciers rivers of slowly moving solid ice.
groundwater water that is found in the rocks under the surface of the Earth.
hydroelectric a way of making electricity by using fast-flowing water.
Ice Age a time when much of the world became very cold and ice covered large parts of the world.
irrigation a way of bringing water to dry areas from rivers and lakes so that crops can be grown.
larvae the second stage in the life of an insect between the egg and the adult.
levees high earth walls built along the banks of a river to stop flooding.
meander the action of a river wandering through a valley.

moraine earth and stones left behind by a glacier.

mud flats a piece of marshy land made by the build-up of mud near a river mouth.

overshot wheel a water-wheel turned by water falling on it from above.

pilgrimage a journey to a special or holy place.

polluted land or water that is spoiled or poisoned.

predators animals that live by hunting and eating other animals.

prey an animal that is hunted and eaten by other animals for food.

rain forest thick dense forest in the tropics where it is very hot and wet.

rapids a part of the river that flows very fast over rocks. The water is usually shallow.

reach a stage of a river.

reservoir a lake built up behind a dam. A reservoir is used for collecting and storing water.

silt a mixture of sand and mud carried along and then dropped by a river.

sluice gates gates in dams that can be opened to let water through or closed to hold the water back.

source the place where a river begins.

springs places where underground water comes to the surface. Springs often trickle out through cracks in the side of mountains or hills.

tributaries streams or rivers that flow into a larger river.

tropical something to do with or coming from the tropics, which are hot damp parts of the world near the Equator.

turbines wheels with many curved blades, which are turned by water or gas.

undershot wheel a water-wheel that is turned by water pushing against it from below.

untreated sewage waste matter from sewers that has not had chemicals added to it to remove the poisons it contains.

vapor a gas or cloud of tiny droplets of water.

water cycle the movement of water from the air to the ground and ocean and back to the air.

Index

algae 14
Amazon River 22, 36, 37

banks 10, 23, 31, 33
barges 23, 31, 32
bridges 23

canals 19, 41
chemicals 44, 45
crater lake 39

Darling River 35
deltas 13, 26, 28, 29, 33
dike 19
drainage 19

erosion 8, 11
estuary 13
evaporation 7

floodplain 12, 29
fresh water 5, 37

Ganges 28, 29

glaciers 38
Great Lakes 25, 40, 41
groundwater 5, 7

hydroelectricity 21, 26, 35

Ice Age 38
irrigation 35

Lake Baikal 25
Lake Kariba 42
Lake Malawi 42
Lake Tanganyika 42, 43
Lake Victoria 42
Lake Volta 25
larvae 14
levees 18

Mississippi River 30, 31
mud flats 13
Murray River 34

Niagara Falls 9
Nile River 5, 24, 26–27

pollution 44, 45
predators 16

rain forest 36
rapids 8
Rhine 32, 33
Rhur 33
riverbed 8

silt 12, 13, 26, 30
Snowy Mountain Project 35
springs 8
St. Lawrence River 41
St. Lawrence Seaway 41
steamboats 31, 35

tributaries 8
turbines 21

Varanasi 28

water cycle 6
water–wheels 20
waterfall 9

Yangtze–Kiang River 22

Acknowledgments
The Publishers wish to thank the following organizations for their invaluable assistance in the preparation of this book.
Australian Information Service, London
Canadian High Commission

Photographic credits
(t=top b=bottom l=left r=right)
Cover: Robert Harding Picture Library; title page Robert Harding Picture Library
4 Ed Lawrenson; 5 ZEFA; 8 The Hutchison Library; 9, 10 ZEFA; 11 South American Pictures; 12t The Hutchison Library; 12b 13 ZEFA; 16 John Lythgoe/Seaphot; 17 Jonathan Scott/Seaphot; 18 Australian Information Service; 19, 20, 21 ZEFA; 22 The Hutchison Library; 23 David George/Seaphot; 26 The Hutchison Library; 27t Douglas Dickens; 27b ZEFA; 28 Douglas Dickens; 29t, 29b The Hutchison Library; 30 ZEFA; 31 Douglas Dickens; 32t, 32b, 33 ZEFA; 34 ANT/NHPA; 34/35 Australian Information Service; 36t, 36b, 37 South American Pictures; 39t Alex Williams/Seaphot; 39b ZEFA; 41t Canadian High Commission; 41b Douglas Dickens; 42, 43 The Hutchison Library; 44 ZEFA; 45 David George/Seapahot